For Ned

Merry Christmas, 1977

Aunt Judy
Julie
Joana

PRAIRIE CHRISTMAS

PRAIRIE CHRISTMAS

Written and Illustrated
By JAMES RICE

SHOAL CREEK PUBLISHERS, INC.

P. O. BOX 9737   AUSTIN, TEXAS 78766

FIRST EDITION

Library of Congress Cataloging in Publication Data
Rice, James, 1934–
Prairie Christmas

SUMMARY: Two lonely cowboys have a mysterious visitor on Christmas Eve.
[1. Santa Claus—Poetry.   2. Christmas poetry]
I. Title.
PZ8.3.R36Pr   811'.5'4   77-14121
ISBN 0-88319-034-6

LITHOGRAPHED AND BOUND IN THE UNITED STATES OF AMERICA

In that sod shanty shack
    far from home, warmth and care
Shivered two lonely cowboys,
    such a scraggly pair.

'Twas a cold Christmas eve
      on the Southwestern plain
And the North wind was blowin'
      through a broke winderpane.

In that sod shanty shack
    far from home, warmth and care
Shivered two lonely cowboys,
    such a scraggly pair.

They crowded the farplace
    where the flames flickered low
From smoldering embers
    that heated too slow.

Then a knock at the door
   and a bang on the wall —
Over the sound of the storm
   they heard a voice call,

"Please open the door
    and let me come in;
I'm near froze to death
    and chilled to the skin."

The door was unbolted
　　and then opened wide
And a fat li'l ole man
　　jumped quickly inside.

There was frost on his whiskers
　　and ice hung from his nose;
He shivered and shook
　　from his head to his toes.

In spite of discomfort
　　he didn't complain.
His expression was jolly
　　as he paused to explain,

"I was movin' this cargo
and making good time;
I'd covered the country
from desert to pine,

"Till I crossed the border
    to this panhandle land
And a Southwestern norther
        commenced stirring the sand.

"The temperature dropped
    more'n a hunnert degrees;
My team soon fled North
    where they'd less likely freeze."

The old cowman had doubts
    'bout the strange little man
But in Southwest tradition
    he put out his hand.

"You can shake off your boots;
    you're welcome to stay
Or we can help ya
    to be on your way."

The answer came quickly
　　with a twinkle of eye,
"I got many a mile yet
　　'fore the sun hits the sky.

"Could you find me a team
　　(I gladly will pay)
Then point my nose South
　　and I'll be on my way."

"The only critters we have
    that could pull a full load
Are the ornery longhorns
    and they'd have to be showed.

"They ain't ever been hitched
    to a wagon with reins;
They'd be too much trouble —
    they're a mite short on brains."

They made an odd threesome
    as they went out on the range —
The old cowhand and the youngster
    and the old man so strange.

They saddled three broncs
    in the dark freezing night;
With cold stiffened fingers
    they made the cinch tight.

While roping the longhorns
　　　they bumped and they stumbled
And numerous times
　　　from their hosses they tumbled.

It took all three working
an hour or more
To hitch up the wagon
in two rows of four.

The longhorns at first
refused to obey,
When the strange little man
tried to get under way.

Then one lifted his head
    and gave out a bellow
And the rest one by one
    they started to follow.

The longhorns were straining
and pulling together;
They built up their speed
then just like a feather —

On a strong gust of wind
their feet gave a bound
Then man, wagon and longhorns
all at once left the ground!

The old cowboy and youngster
    stared up in surprise,
A trick of the storm,
    too much wind in the eyes —

Those were their thoughts
    as they looked at the sky;
Any fool knew darn well
    that such things cannot fly.

The young cowboy grumbled
    as they moved toward the shack,
But the old one stayed quiet
    pert' near all the way back.

They reached the sod shanty
and opened the door
And they couldn't believe
what they saw on the floor.

Two pairs of new boots
    with spurs made of silver,
With a note but no clue
    as to who was the giver.

They made out the words
    in the dim farplace light:
"MERRY CHRISTMAS TO ALL
    AND TO ALL A GOOD NIGHT!"